Sufjan

poems by

Hannah Larrabee

Finishing Line Press
Georgetown, Kentucky

Sufjan

Copyright © 2017 by Hannah Larrabee
ISBN 978-1-63534-122-5 First Edition
All rights reserved under International and Pan-American Copyright Conventions.
No part of this book may be reproduced in any manner whatsoever without written permission from the publisher, except in the case of brief quotations embodied in critical articles and reviews.

ACKNOWLEDGMENTS

Grateful acknowledgement is made to *Mass Poetry* for featuring "Praying Mantis" online.

Publisher: Leah Maines

Editor: Christen Kincaid

Cover Art: Bárbara Ana Gómez

Author Photo: Allison Mascolo

Cover Design: Elizabeth Maines

Printed in the USA on acid-free paper.
Order online: www.finishinglinepress.com
also available on amazon.com

Author inquiries and mail orders:
Finishing Line Press
P. O. Box 1626
Georgetown, Kentucky 40324
U. S. A.

Table of Contents

Praying Mantis 1

Even the Earth Will Perish and the Universe Give Way 3

Ursa Minor 4

In the Shadow of the Cross 5

Futile Devices 7

Fourth of July 8

Year of the Sheep: Iceland 9

Climate Change 10

I'm Sorry the Worst Has Arrived 11

Pangaea 12

All of Me Wants All of You 13

Fortune-Teller 14

Be Kind Rewind 15

Collisions 16

To Be Alone with You 17

Concerning the UFO Sighting Near Franconia Notch 18

Raise Your Red Flag 20

Neptune 21

Vesuvius 22

Impossible Soul 23

Notes 25

> And I am speechless
> All that I've said to get it right
> And I am confident
> You ran off with it all
>
> —Sufjan Stevens, *Mercury*

PRAYING MANTIS

Oh I can tell you, terrible sting, how easily someone can turn
away, but don't take it all to heart.

No one else is looking for that dark energy,
that thing that holds this all together, even here.

*

Last night the wind kicked up through the window
and left the wine glasses chattering, hanging from their stems
like upside down tulips.

*

Now a virus chases my beanbag cells. It is gaining speed.
I am losing.

*

I look for something inside Snapple bottle caps
but find only useless facts like, "The Praying Mantis
is the only insect that can turn its head."

Well, it also decapitates its lovers. So, there's that.

*

You keep up with your beautiful words.
You set a hard line for the horizon.

*

But I am in love with the moon backlit
by only a sliver of light, enough to reveal
the whole dark mess.

In the end, I want it closer.

I am not the Praying Mantis, stiff-armed
and sharp-edged.

I am the night grass (the whole
busy world). I am the way it feels
on bare feet.

I am the way I fall into it.
I am the way of falling.

EVEN THE EARTH WILL PERISH AND THE UNIVERSE GIVE WAY

Old man rocking back and forth
on the train, ocean of his own
turmoil, we'll call him… seasick…
is repeating: *I'm just like you.*
I'm just like you.

And he is.

7% cowardice.

93% star fuel.

URSA MINOR

What else matters when I am out walking under stars,
the way I used to sleep: those glowing stickers that never came
off my ceiling, the heart ached so much the roof gave way,
brought the night sky inside. Slow sediment, something must have
changed *my love for you it bruised it bruised my will* and not in the way
of overnight things, it was the river at the mouth of the ocean: all panic
you touched me inside of my cage beneath my shirt your hands and I'm sorry,
it seems I must have fallen, Ursa Minor, little ladle, bring me back
to the surface, taste me for brine, what is there to add? Or, like a fish
that does not measure, throw me back.

IN THE SHADOW OF THE CROSS

I'm wondering how often it is
that foreign light

touches down, an unidentified
flying object

landing in the shadow of the cross.
And if they were

to ask, we could say the cross
sprung up from the ground,

that we have no recollection
of what it is for

until we are reminded how many
have died

on its scaffolding. I want to say:
you can't come down

yet, the room isn't ready, I've not
done the dishes,

and anyway, we can't share a cup
of tea, properly,

until 4pm, and can't you see that
Venus

is sitting atop Jupiter in the night sky
like a parakeet on a shoulder?

I am feeling nonsense, like I could
roll planets around

between my fingers. Come down,
come down, when I am

picking berries, when I am stained
vaguely human.

FUTILE DEVICES

Having witnessed a woman drop to her knees, collecting
the scattered papers of a stranger.

Having been heart-shoved against a locker,
high school dizzy.

Having thought: *I am not that kind of person*, spilling into
what kind of person am I not?

Having no words, futile devices, for the only-color
of your eyes.

Having said it plain as day, now back to night,
to the geometry of dandelions turned ghost.

Having loved these ever-living thoughts of you:
comet tails, throat seeds.

FOURTH OF JULY

How do you know so well the death that has come
for me, in words, burden of what cannot be captured,
the feeling of fireflies in the field, their bright reluctance
to the camera shutter. The Milky Way arches over us
and we lack patience, the ability to gather light. I still
cannot say what I felt, so I stumble over the only thing
that comes to me. I have abandoned this body, this
beautiful organism. Here in the dark, awaiting fireworks,
I know you are happy where you are. There is a need
for your body, which you felt once, even when it could
not be carried. On separate days I have missed my fins,
my feathers, my modest beak, my goat eyes. I am too
loosely bound to this place. The fire has taken all
my undergrowth, more than once, a Tillamook Burn.
And I, too, escape the shutter. I, too, have been fearful.

YEAR OF THE SHEEP: ICELAND

A language that pelts
like rain.

A driver who drives too fast
through lava fields.

Green lichen on stone.

Impossible photographs.

The Geysir.
The growling stomach.

What we have waited for
has waited for us.

Grows impatient.

I have taken a handful of stone,
lined my pockets.

Veins straight to the earth
to draw from.

CLIMATE CHANGE

I've been thinking
again, the way you fold
into the inner fabric
of my brain, how else
can I say something
like this to you when
you don't care to know
the frustrating nearness
of strangers, how this
all could have been
predicted without
someone there to read
my palms. Whatever
this is, it is also an unfair
equation, like our search
for another planet
in the 11th hour and 59th
minute, and all heartbreak
aside, it turns out
I am bottomless
clear water
fissure
the ocean acidifies,
300 parts per million
is just too crowded,
and oh how saturated,
how ashamed.

I'M SORRY THE WORST HAS ARRIVED

Each layered measure of earth and dust,
strata and shale, you

rest your elbows on the bar, gorgeous,
and so I watch for a moment

from a distance, what's the rush?
You are there waiting,

you are where you said you'd be.

Under a steady rain, the walk back to my car
was not enough

to clear me, not enough to best the knowledge
held under my tongue.

In the parking lot, alarm lights flicker from dashboards
like spinning satellites—

measured warnings, though they do not intend harm.

But I have already broken all the rules of your
surroundings.

I have spilled myself like the long shadows of clouds
over mountains.

PANGAEA

If we were once all together, and if we were then split apart, there can be no other word for this but longing. Thread a mind together in code, neurons made by our own fingers; the artificial, the intelligent, will never be born with this. That love is not an index, that the orbit bends with the strength of gravity, with the lack of gravity.
That it can be the same love discovered again and again, like children digging for fossils in backyards: imagination ensures they will find them. And I believe the harsh world will hold its tongue, just then, when you reach into your pockets and come up with all you have.

ALL OF ME WANTS ALL OF YOU

If there were leaves of me, I would want you
to graze them with your hand.

Why can't I be enough places at once that this
cannot be helped?

Of course, I would recognize the difference
and ache to be human again.

Your nails glancing my inner wrist.

FORTUNE-TELLER

Madam Marie, I can't set foot inside your store.

Seer, fortune-teller, who else but me wants me to know
I have let them down?

Wouldn't you prefer to share a cup of tea?

We could sit together in that way
strangers share a bench waiting for the train.

Madam Marie, we just passed by Pluto.

Yes, yes Mercury in retrograde… but lately I have chosen
a pendulum to heed its heavier advice,

I have read my own cards and they are profound:
silence carved like petroglyphs on stone.

Madam Marie, I once shared a booth with the only
person who seemed to matter.

It didn't work out, as you know.

Madam Marie, would you hold my hands
which have gone too long unheld?

And how much will this cost me?

BE KIND REWIND

Now I am a forest
shriveling to desert,
the pinwheel of a fern
backing into ground,
my legs scrambling
backward, VHS says
BE KIND REWIND
it does not hurt
to be the occasional
fool, *be still and know
your sign*, let the scene
play out as it will:
one wall—a monument,
several taxis—a silence
and *we stayed a long long
time*, until it became
obvious what we were
not good at, until
it became obvious
your smile remained
the same, though
*we stayed a long
long time.*

COLLISIONS

It takes a lot to want to touch, not talk, not reiterate, just touch,
as it happens in those subzero particle accelerator chambers
of the Large Hadron Collider, and the fallout: atom ink splattered
on computer canvas, is, essentially, all that is left behind of our
conversation—vague as a solar flare, static on the line only
for a moment. What carries over, anyway, when the body is ash,
is gifted underground? Is it the soul looping in those massive metal
chambers, bicyclists oblivious above ground, pursuing their own
days on quaint Geneva streets? I want to be given a choice to be
two things at once, like particles and waves, and if given the choice
then how many times has this happened before? And is that why
I feel so homesick around you—memory a collision, then waves
moving away as they do, getting bigger as they do, forgetting
what it was like to be near you, to be particles? No matter, you
are the bicyclist above ground, having assumed the worst of me
for reasons that touch and burn, skin at subzero. You will not allow
yourself to be charted. You are back to particle, coupled and renamed,
while I am bound to waves, repeating into oblivion.

TO BE ALONE WITH YOU

Those common winter companions,
chickadees,

slow their hearts and lungs in sleep,
but their bodies give away

no secrets, sitting solitary on a wire.

As the Christmas Eve candles are lit
within the pews,

the harpist plucks at strings with hands
that become beaks

carrying off sound.

I have come here to forage at the ground.
If you were to take

a new body, I would still recognize
the long shadow

of your shoulder.

CONCERNING THE UFO SIGHTING NEAR FRANCONIA NOTCH
After the alleged abduction of Betty and Barney Hill in New Hampshire, September 1961.

I don't need you to believe me.

Just tell me how the car traveled
35 miles without us driving,

tell me exactly how the vibration felt
inside our Chevy Bel Air,

the rugged stature of the White Mountains
all around us.

I'll say it again: there were no stars.

How could they take away the night
my lips stitched

to whatever was left of language?

I drew you a map and still you have
not found

the place between those distant stars.

I don't care about the size of the object,
the direction

of its rotation, how my mind went
to something else

my dreams too, or the useless things
I know somehow.

If you want what I have, take it.
That's what I tried to tell you,

what difference does it make *who*
is not listening if *no one* is listening?

Play the recordings again. No,
that is not my voice.

Tell me, do you have room for me
here

to rest my head? And if I have been
returned,

why can't I come home?

RAISE YOUR RED FLAG

No one ever affixes a label to silence.

Where else have you given me to look,
the bottom of a river, the curve around the bend?

It was filament encased in glass, a muted burn.

But we whispered in such a way that we were there:
circling each other in orbit,

paying close attention to the strawberries
on countertops, the shared salad, the red flag.

No need to raise it now.

NEPTUNE

Fond as I am
of that blue orb,

frigid as an ice pack,
it listens in

on the conversations
between planets

too shy to say a word.
Olbers' paradox

says nothing is static,
especially not

the universe, and darkness
is its only proof.

I want to set foot
in Andromeda.

It is as real as any
feeling I've had,

so *forgive me for feeling it
out for myself*

because I have wished
out loud

and it brought me
nothing.

VESUVIUS
> *fire of fire, fall on me now*
> *as I favor the ghost*

They drag a lion through mud in Tbilisi.

Jaw of charcoal.

The river is still rising.

Lions swept from the zoo,

prisoners who left the cell for the chamber.

How much darker is the universe?

Stampede of shadow.

Need has never been your problem.

Lead me through the narrow space that opens

to Chauvet Cave.

Light a fire on the floor.

Nothing more or less required

to come alive.

IMPOSSIBLE SOUL

I stand in the metal joints
of the train

junction of railcar bones
headphones in

unable to block it all
forget everything I know

for a language

that makes sense
of these invisible filaments

that draw me to you

forget everything I know
for the language

of neutrinos
rolling off the tongue

passing though body
and rock

taking on nothing
and I am

inching toward
all things romantic again

a billion neutrinos pass
through my fingernail

every second but a smile
is the mystery

we can't solve?

Love as old as
a Galapagos turtle

its nails the same age
as the universe

forget everything I know
for the feeling

I am bailing out a rowboat
in another place

because I said the words
go live the life

you should
in a dream

because I said the words
I love you

when you were leaving

because a comet burned
up on its way

and fell to earth
in pieces.

NOTES:

All of these poems draw inspiration from songs by Sufjan Stevens, and that inspiration includes: tone, sound, lyrics (in italics), and other aspects inherent in filtering one artistic medium through another.

The songs that influence each of the poems are listed here in order:

"Praying Mantis"—The Predatory Wasp of the Palisades is Out to Get Us! (*Illinois*)
"Even the Earth Shall Perish and the Universe Give Way"—song by the same name (*Silver & Gold*)
"Ursa Minor"—The Owl and the Tanager (*All Delighted People*)
"In the Shadow of the Cross"—No Shade in the Shadow of the Cross (*Carrie & Lowell*)
"Futile Devices"—song by the same name (*The Age of Adz*)
"Fourth of July"—song by the same name (*Carrie & Lowell*)
"Year of the Sheep: Iceland"—Year of the Sheep (*Enjoy Your Rabbit*)
"Climate Change"—Romulus (*Michigan*)
"I'm Sorry the Worst Has Arrived"—I Walked (*The Age of Adz*)
"Pangea"—John My Beloved (*Carrie & Lowell*)
"All of Me Wants All of You"—song by the same name (*Carrie & Lowell*)
"Fortune-Teller"—The Seer's Tower (*Illinois*)
"Be Kind Rewind"—In the Devil's Territory (*Seven Swans*)
"Collisions"—Mercury (part of the Planetarium Project)
"To Be Alone with You"—song by the same name (*Seven Swans*)
"Concerning the UFO Sighting Near Franconia Notch"—Concerning the UFO Sighting Near Highland, Illinois (*Illinois*)
"Raise Your Red Flag"—Blue Bucket of Gold (*Carrie & Lowell*)
"Neptune"—Neptune (part of the Planetarium Project)
"Vesuvius"—song by the same name (*The Age of Adz*) *references floods that swept through a zoo in Tbilisi, Georgia in June 2015
"Impossible Soul"—song by the same name (*The Age of Adz*)

Hannah **Larrabee** is the author of *Virgo* (Finishing Line Press, 2009), Sufjan (Finishing Line Press), and *Murmuration* (forthcoming from Seven Kitchens Press). She was recently chosen by NASA to participate in their call for artists, allowing her to view the James Webb Space Telescope in person before it launches in 2018. She's had poems appear in *Rock & Sling, The Fourth River, HOUSEGUEST, Printer's Devil Review,* among others. Hannah teaches college writing and works for a technology company in Boston. She has an M.F.A. in Creative Writing from the University of New Hampshire.

www.ingramcontent.com/pod-product-compliance
Lightning Source LLC
LaVergne TN
LVHW041517070426
835507LV00012B/1636